MW01539178

LIGHT.

A Journal of Photography & Poetry

FINISHING

FALL 2019

FOUNDER & MANAGING EDITOR
Jennifer Drucker

POETRY EDITOR
Manny Blackscher

MAILING ADDRESS

PO BOX 420, SMITHTOWN, NY 11787

WEBSITE

WWW.LIGHT-JOURNAL.COM

Light Journal ISSN 2473-6147 (Online)/ISSN 2470-7732 (Print) is published four times a year by Focus Publishing, Inc. P.O. Box 420, Smithtown, NY 11787, e-mail: editor@light-journal.com. Digital and print issues are available from our website: www.light-journal.com/subscribe. ©2019 LIGHT Journal. All Rights Reserved. Reproduction in whole or in part without permission is prohibited. Cover Image: *NC Airport* by Jennifer Drucker

IN THIS ISSUE | FINISHING

A Note From the Editor

"A thing is complete when you can let it be"
-Gita Bellin

When I began this adventure three years ago, my goal was to curate some of the best poetry and photography under one cover. Curating the two mediums was challenging, a challenge I passionately pursued along with Manny. We received thousands of submissions from all over the world. Each of you, whether you subscribed, sent notes of appreciation, or submitted the beautiful work we relied on for each issue, became part of this journey.

What started as just a small idea from one person, became the collective work of hundreds and I am so proud of what we have accomplished together. It is bittersweet as I announce it is time to 'let it be'.

Thank you for your support of *Light*. While this is our last issue, printed copies of all twelve issues will be available to order in perpetuity from our website www.light-journal.com

Warm regards,

Jennifer Drucker
Founder & Managing Editor

JESSICA MICHAEL | *Water & Ghosts I*

LOUIS GALLO | *Snapshots*

The one face you won't find
in those hundreds of early photos
of me and the family, I then a child,
posing with my sister and mother, is Dad,
an absence, a hole, missing
yet so much more urgently present
than any of us. Sometimes
you see a smudge at the corner,
his thumb, but always you feel
a presence, the banker of scenes
and spirit behind the lens.
Dad no longer takes the pictures
because this time he's really gone.
Not a single fingerprint.
I depress the button now. And
again, the one person you won't find
in the hundreds of later photos
of my family is me. My wife
and two children smile, wave,
smirk, pose, croak "cheese"
so often they crave relief.
And me, sometimes you'll find
my thumb, sometimes, nothing at all.

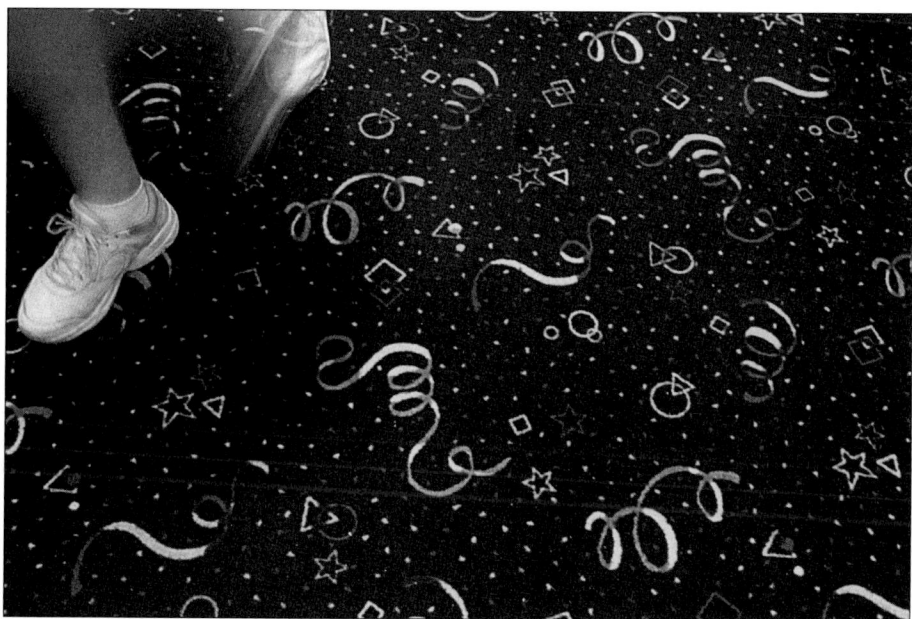

DAVE MAGYAR | *Fascination*

JACKIE HUPPENTHAL | *Lupine*

J.J. STEINFELD | *And Dream, on Occasion, of Namelessness*

If you breathe in a colour
a colour without an accurate name
a colour wanting more from its name
and dream, on occasion,
of namelessness
and encompassing many colours
magically in one
a magician learning
to make colours appear and disappear
amidst the cantankerous rabbits
who feel betrayed
now that the colours
are dancing all over the stage
the way rabbits used to
in the old days
when madness and mischief
were all the rage
will you become whole again
like a beautiful colour?

to make them laugh
e ri - der vuo -
once
le
lingeringly
(violently)
Opt.
You must a - muse
Tra - mu - ta in laz -
Laugh through
Ri - di
verg-ing
so dal
mean - ing
pren - do
roar!
rà!
the
to,
mad
li
dream
e so -
With
Men-
All
A
the love that is dy - ing,
tuo a - mo - re in - fran - to!
murmuring
for
no;
the light
nel guar -
for
af -
Pa - gliac - cio,
Pa - gliac - cio,
Ann
Hart!
A
On with your cos - tume
Ve - sti la giub - ba
Play a part!
Re - ci - tar!
show them
u - na s
Life
Ed
The crowd will
La gen - te
pay you
pa - ga
in
tut-
grease paint and pow - der,
fac-cia in - fa - ri - na.
love you
vo - glio a
love!
mo!
you!
ra!
Copyright
A. Dupont
And yet
Ep - pur
Broadly, with ecstasy
be - tray you,
lom - bi - na,

ANN HART | *For Pagliaccio*

J.J. STEINFELD | *Thinking of Words*

I went to bed
thinking the word infinite
and awoke with the word finite
rolling around my thoughts
like a sinister jester
performing not for mischief
but for wickedness.
Forget the previous image:
let me try again—
like a bemused deity
who wants to offer more
but always winds up
short changing
even the happiest
and the saddest
who think of words
during hopeful nights
and forsaken mornings.

LOUIS STAEBLE | *Untitled*

LOUIS STAEBLE | *Untitled*

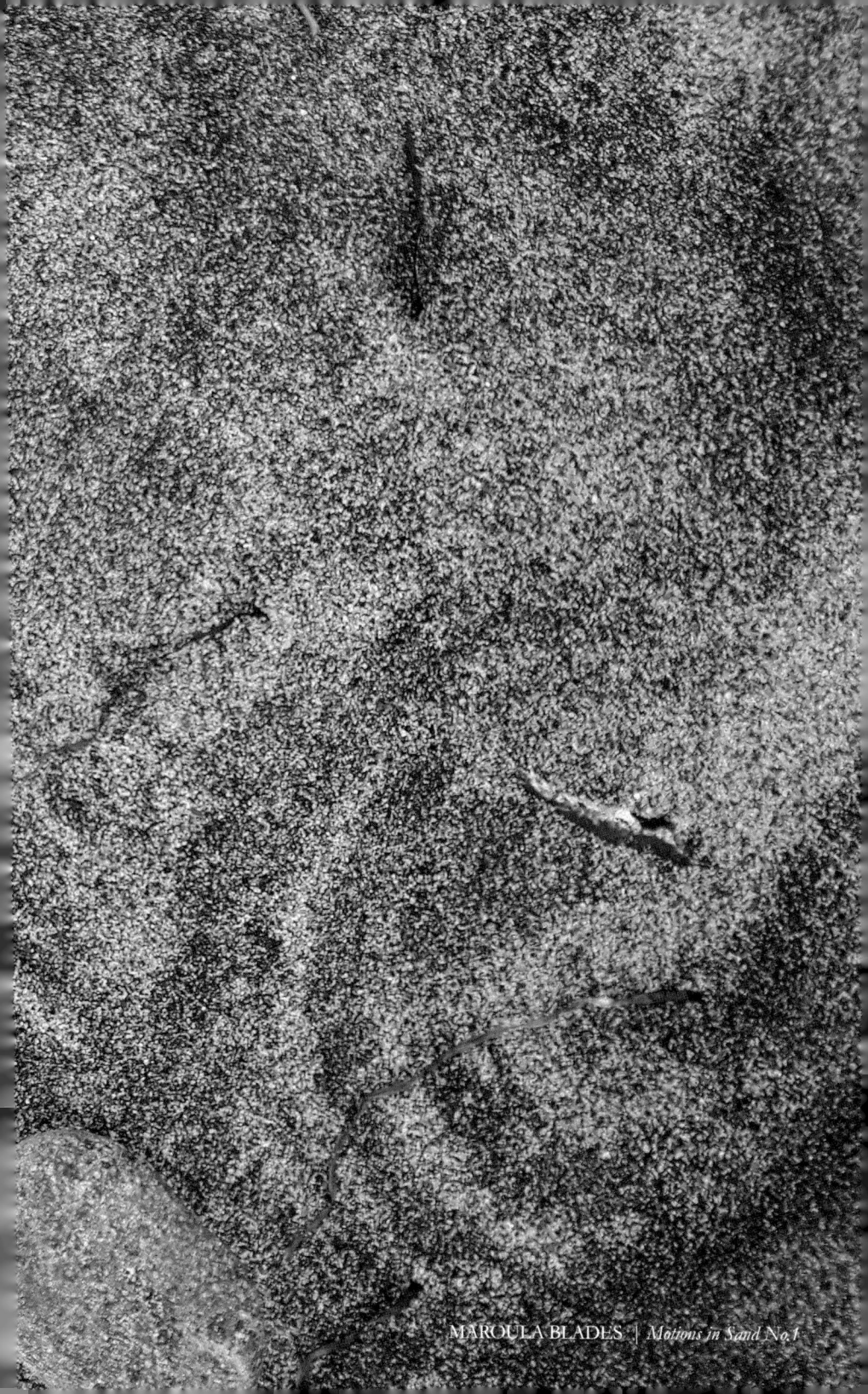

MAROULA BLADES | *Motions in Sand No.1*

SILVINO GONZALEZ | *Untitled*

GENE HYDE | *The Anthropocene Dweller Speaks of Rivers*
"My soul has grown deep like the rivers" - Langston Hughes

I once knew rivers
Both bold and meek, all aflow
Across the green globe.

I long for rivers
To again grow deep; my soul
Untroubled, reposed.

I dream of rivers,
Gushing creeks of melted snow:
Threads in Gaia's robes.

GAIL GOEPFERT | *Portfolio Unfinished*
[Self-portrait 1954] Vivian Maier

Was it a pawn shop window
where she took that 1950's selfie,
her reflection
through chain-link
in the silver shine
of a serving tray on display.
A flat cap of lifeless hair
on an angular face.
Her nose large and beak-like
in distortion.
Eyes no more than lids.
Fossilized on film.

Given life only in shiny things.

I.

I snap every angle,
as if the shutter's open/close
will make this six-foot spike
corpse flower, titan arum,
cocooned in a leaf-like spathe.
Nicknamed Alice—
the botanic garden's current pride
and joy. Visitors circle, gawk.
When it opens, expect the smell
of rotting meat—the morbid appeal
of a highway smashup.

II.

Outside the Striporama,
Vivian shoots
a grandiose poster advertising
Lili St. Cyr, and *Georgia* and *Rosita,*
their last names veiled
by a fleshy woman,
darkly-clothed, scarf
to black tie shoes, standing
on her head, pant legs
to her knees, hands
gripping spider-like,
the city's dog-eared pavement.

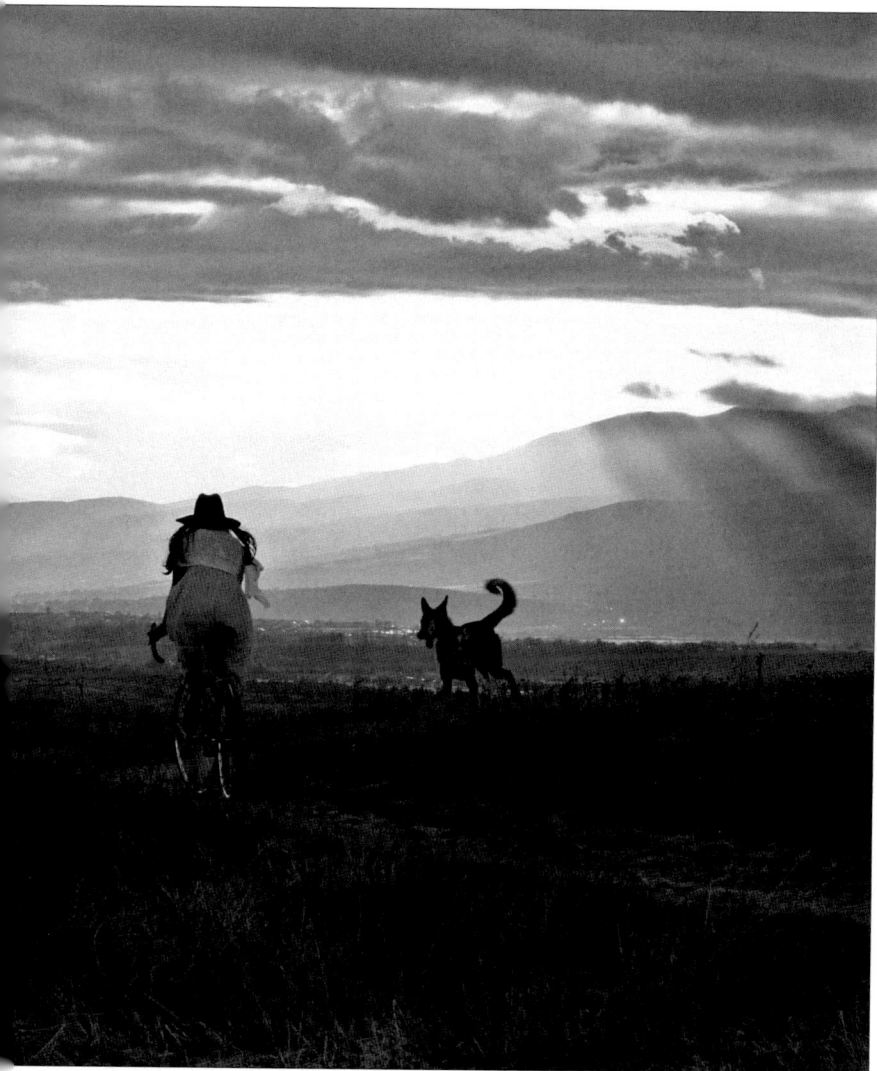

SABRINA GUITART | *Summer Dusk*

KARLA LINN MERRIFIELD
How to Edit a Loser Lover

~~Strikethrough~~ his blue October-sky eyes.
//////-stitch shut his teasing Irish grin.
█████ out the silky pelt of his wrestler's pecs and abs.
Wing-ding that man's Astroglided grade-A equipment—
♍□♍& ♋■♎ ♌♋●●◆.

But! Stet those firm twin globes of his fine ass
you once fingernailed, bruised, and smacked in passion.
I'll lend you my Imelda Marco collection of shoes,
every single come-fuck-me stiletto I own,
to kick that gorgeous sorry butt and his cluelessness

from here to West Hoboken and beyond.

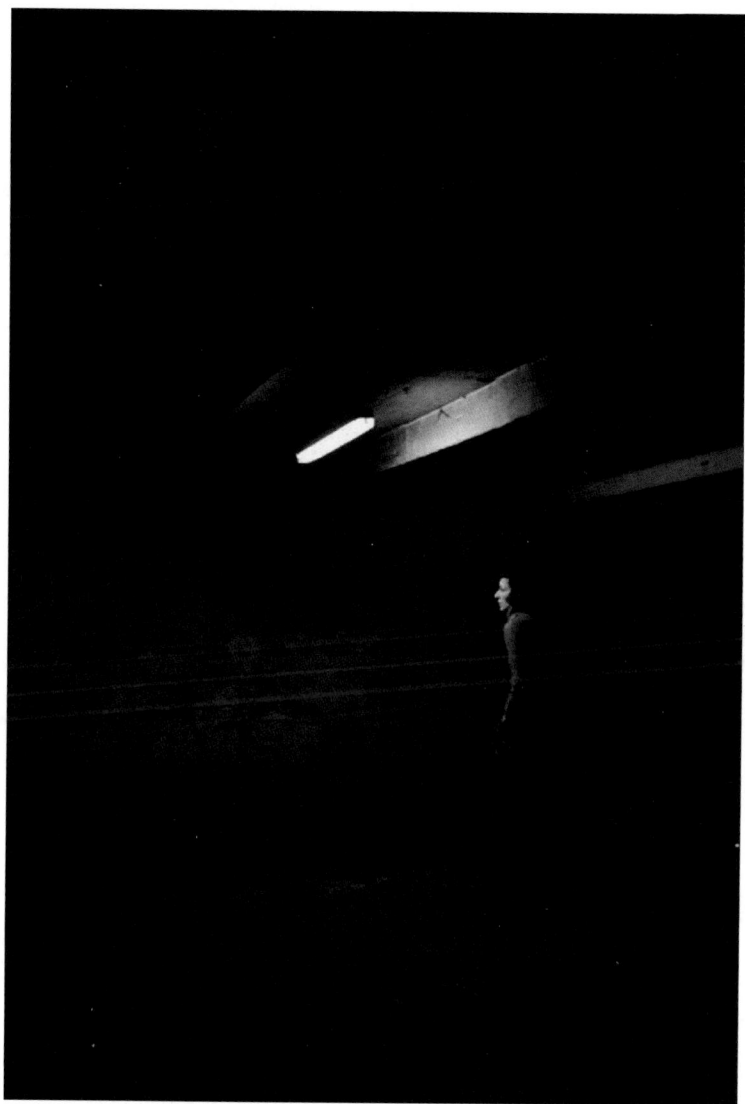

JULIE PEIFFER | *Cash in that Raincheck*

LUCAS SHEPHERD | *Inactive Duty IV*

I came home with ten
thousand dollars saved up.

In one year my uniform
didn't fit. We grow into

the lives we live, maybe.
On the road home I slept

over at my KIA'd cousin's house
and left early the next morn

-ing. His parents—my aunt
and uncle—watched me go.

I was still on terminal
leave until Valentine's Day,

I was twenty-five
years old, I was a
-
shamed,
definitely.

I never suffered enough;
I wasn't there there.

Sometimes I stop and count
the years since, sometimes

I stop and count the aircraft, fighters
and gunships, trips across the flightline.

When my cousin died over
-seas he was twenty-six.

In one year my
uniform didn't fit.

LUCAS SHEPHERD | *Drone Attack in Walmart Toy Aisle*

I am holding my three-year-old
        daughter in the toy aisle of our local
        Walmart, staring

at a G.I. Joe-knockoff
        action playset with three-inch
        figurines and a military jeep

and a small drone aircraft.
        I want to tell her the funny story
        about my work with drone aircraft

but it's one of those had-to-have
        -been-there stories and anyway
        it's not so much funny

as sad. Whenever my three-year-old
        hurts herself, a skinned knee
        or stubbed toe, I try

to make her laugh. I make funny
        faces or fart noises with my mouth.
        The way I conflate

these emotions, who knows
        —maybe she would get a kick
        out of my drone story after all.

TARA TROIANO | *Untitled*

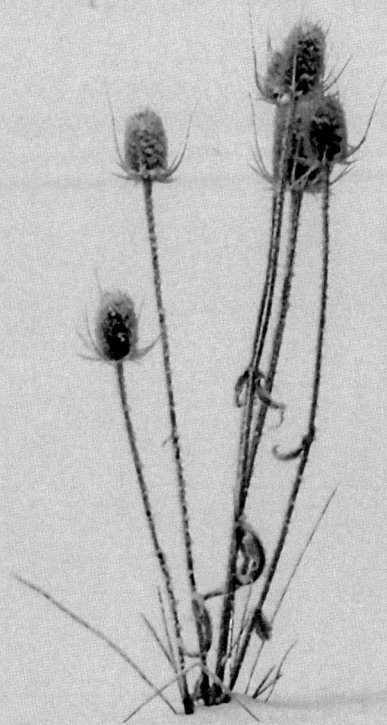

LYNDA WRIGHT | *St. Russo's Fire*

MARY K O'MELVENY | *The Fire This Time*

Desert boundaries shape shift like werewolves.
Sometimes, they move slow as a seed unfolding
to blossom. Other days, it happens quick
as a knife slash or a Bedouin tent
folding at dawn. Even in rain, oases
shrivel up like belated apologies.

Saharan sands will surely land in Kansas.
As they expand to every crevice,
sift through kaftans across continents,
settle in hair and eyes, will we all sink,
parched, blinded, survival skills swept away?
Before too long, we could become Mars.

As fables are told, retold, voices slip slide
across barren ground, nestle in cracks
grown wide as riverbeds. We never saw it
coming, someone claims as dust drifts down
from ancient stars to lands where villages
once glistened under rays from a red sun.

LYNN WHITE | *Shall I Go Gently*

I've always been indecisive
and I'm still undecided
but soon
I will have to choose
whether to build my ship,
and furnish it
comfortably
and sail with you
gently
into the dark
into oblivion
gently
or to rage and fight
scratch and bite
kick and scream
so that you have to drag me
to where I will not follow
gently
into oblivion
into the darkness
the inevitability
of the end
whichever way I choose.

JENNIE MACDONALD | *Untitled*

JUDY DECROCE | *A Perfect Storm*

Coming on like old vengeance
subtracting the hours
subtracting the shore

high winds at high tide
and, battering rain too.

(What else?)
as the dance floor clears

Nauset beaten back into history.

The land leaving
The rollers coming
— a tango
of geographic proportions.

Sea and dunes partnered
to a vanishing point.

ANTONI OOTO | *Landward*

under great immensity and distant
                        at the lowest point of sky
a gull leans windward   light to dark

as headwinds keep the flag busy
grey afternoon   narrow water
a red triangle reads the channel

                    weather gains attention
a summer storm hesitates

cracks to a finger of light
a mat of stillness   only waves pawing

          a frame of sand

RUTH HOLZER | *Portail de l'église Saint-Etienne-du-Mont, 1898*
(Eugene Atget photograph)

Rinsed in pure morning light,
the west facade, with its elegant
fluted Corinthian columns
and Romanesque arch capped
by an ornate medallion.
The massive portals are shut.
In a small open doorway to the right
a woman in a coarse apron
is leaning on a wooden crutch.
She regards with a complacent eye
her display of relics and curios.
Customers will come again
after viewing the carved angels,
the saints patient in their niches,
the parapet and decorated pinnacles,
the flying buttresses, the slender bell tower
and the pediment frieze:
the moment of martyrdom,
the stoning of Stephen.

RUTH HOLZER | *Florist, Boulevard St. Michel, 1898*
(Eugene Atget photograph)

Bowler-hatted idlers on the quai.
The coachman asleep in his coach.
A woman surrounded by bunches of flowers
and long-spouted watering cans
sits quietly near the kiosk
in the shadow of the plane tree,
plying her small trade
of lilacs and lavender
and sad violets nobody wants.

L.R. HARVEY | *the farmer's wife's journal*

You cup my face with spindled hands to kiss
my cheek, leaving red waxy love I wipe
away. Your lacy robe ascends the steps

with regal strides, a train of cream perfume
billowing behind until you slip
inside your door to climb your king-sized throne

and settle in sleep. A child, I creep up stairs
that creak just like your knees. The bathroom door
is old, like everything else, and squeals to scare

the cat. Blue chipping floor is tile-cold,
but I have learned to dodge the slivers
that cut a novice foot, a dance of sorts.

A wisp of loose-robed white, I slide myself
into the middle, right between the mirrors
hung parallel above the facing shelves

of perfume vials and toothpaste tubes, and watch
my thin reflection bouncing back and forth
in endless, smudgy images. The catch

is that you cannot look yourself in the eye
because you'll block the view, but if
you stand just right and twist, you'll tunnel by

on either side until you disappear
in infinite stacking dolls. Back then the trick
was young and fresh, exciting, just like you were.

That woman's husk, today you rest on top
the sheets, a barn-dried sheaf of Autumn corn.
I do not know how much you hear, and stop

to dab your spittled mouth. The walls are bare,
empty of mirrors, but flesh reflects enough.
They say I have your hair.

At 8:13, the solitary oak
outside the kitchen window pulls down the sun
with groping, fibrous fingers. Shadows stroke
the stucco wall in stenciled lines, and on
the counter, store-bought casserole is cold.
His mother snores. He creaks the screened-in door
to slide his bare feet over the concrete stoop
in callous whispers. Outside, the evening air
is soft as puppy's breath. The grass is wet.

His mother's face was wet the day his dad
had went away, wet Carolina sunset
streaks of red on cheeks that he had kissed.
John had moved in that year, a cheshire smile
from cheek to cheek that said "just call me dad,"
but whiskey fists can't hide behind a smile.

Cicada song blankets his lilting stride
across the lawn, his shuffle leaving strokes
of green on cloth of dew. They sing him on
his way out to the road to stand on top
the yellow lines that split the street that splits the town
in two. The paint is cool as kitchen tiles.

That day, his father hooked the tin-roof trailer
behind the red-roof truck, the earthy smell
of split-hoofed cattle mingling with the odor
of burnt tobacco leaf and hay. They'd stood
out by the barn together and watched the geese
fly past the house in waving ribboned strands,
to disappear behind the beechwood trees
that lined the field. His father's algae eyes
spoke longing in the silence. By evening he was gone.

The citrus moon drips down a lemon rind
of evening light that sprinkles him alone,
staring down the road that drops away
behind the distant hill. Tonight, he swears
he too will one day walk the yellow lines
that sink beyond his sight. He'll disappear
to find the land of weary fathers, geese,
and all who feel the world is not a place
                              for staying.

37

JAE CASELLA | *Sunset Watchers on the Cliff*

PHOTOGRAPHY
Featured Portfolio

SUSANA PATRAS | *Pacifica*

Biography

After graduating from the university with a degree in English, Susanna Patras decided to follow a different career path and continued her studies in multimedia and photography. While during the first part of her career she focused on journalism and poetry, a few years ago her interest shifted towards visual arts, in particular graphic design and photography.

POETRY
Featured Collection

KEVIN HIGGINS

Kevin Higgins best-selling first collection, *The Boy With No Face*, was published by Salmon Poetry in 2005 and short-listed for the 2006 Strong Award for Best First Collection by an Irish poet. Kevin's second collection of poems, *Time Gentlemen, Please*, was published in 2008 by Salmon Poetry and his poetry is discussed in *The Cambridge Introduction to Modern Irish Poetry*. His third collection *Frightening New Furniture* was published in 2010 by Salmon and his work also appears in the generation defining anthology *Identity Parade –New British and Irish Poets* (Ed. Roddy Lumsden, Bloodaxe, 2010) and in *The Hundred Years' War: modern war poems* (Ed. Neil Astley, Bloodaxe, April 2014). A collection of Kevin's essays and book reviews, Mentioning The War, was published by Salmon Poetry in 2012. Kevin's poetry has been translated into Greek, Spanish, Turkish, Italian, Japanese, Russian, & Portuguese. His most recent collection of poetry, The Ghost in The Lobby, was published in February 2014, also by Salmon. In 2014 Kevin's poetry was the subject of a paper 'The Case of Kevin Higgins, or, 'The Present State of Irish Poetic Satire' presented by David Wheatley at a Symposium on Satire at the University of Aberdeen. '2016 - The Selected Satires of Kevin Higgins' was published by NuaScéalta earlier this year. A pamphlet of Kevin's political poems *The Minister For Poetry Has Decreed* was published in December by the Culture Matters imprint of the UK based Manifesto Press; *Song of Songs 2:0 - New and Selected Poems* will be published by Salmon in April 2017. His poems have been praised by, among others, Tony Blair's biographer John Rentoul, *Observer* columnist Nick Cohen, and *Sunday Independent* columnist Gene Kerrigan; and have been quoted in *The Daily Telegraph, The Independent,* and *The Daily Mirror.* The Stinging Fly magazine recently described Kevin as "likely the most read living poet in Ireland."

Clump of Cells
after William Blake

You are, at most, a week or two old.
How big will you grow?
Your potential, vast.
For now you're happy
to skulk there, quietly establishing yourself,
elbowing out of your way
those who lack your secret code.

No one knows you've arrived:
two, four, six, eight
secretly becoming a trillion
while they take you with them on picnics
or give you your first taste of gin and tonic,
though you don't yet officially exist.

Everyone knows your name.
It decorates the headed notepaper
of esteemed charities and titles of reports,
some of which, if ever, will be published
with the names redacted and all indentifiers expunged.
Careers and fortunes made doing research into you.

But, for now, you are nothing,
a touch of fatigue,
a vague feeling of discomfort
that's probably a pulled muscle.
The second they know you're here
they'll start sweating
and whispering your name
and stop taking you on picnics.
Even if they succeed in killing you
they'll spend forever looking for signs of you.

Not Yet
after Hans Mangus Enzensberger

I'm sat here heroically
thinking about perhaps having
another buttered fruit scone.
The family animal dozes
on the giant leather sofa
I bought for it. It is not yet
time to commit suicide again.

The galvanised roof
hasn't yet blown off
the shed I inherited
from Mother. The light bulb over
the front door would work,
if I chose to switch it on.
The car alarm
has been silenced for now.

That the evening might finish up
in my favourite restaurant
remains a theoretical possibility.
The scented candle hasn't yet
set the curtains on fire.
And Germany has yet
to be re-partitioned.

I am still in a position
to deny everything.

A hearse comes gleaming
through the evening traffic
with no body in it.

What am I waiting for?

Nothing
after Edward Thomas

The soot of evening tumbles
to Earth, turning the street to nothing.
A mad old women – or what sounds
like a mad old woman – with a voice
trapped down a chimney accuses
the world of once again letting the children
feed a nest load of magpie chicks
to the black cat. The cat, if it exists,
doesn't care, its mouth full of meat
and blue blue feathers. Nothing
is what it was half an hour ago.
The bicycle chained to the lamppost
has ceased to be.
The restaurant is secretly empty
but for a couple who tonight will each
dream they're driving a bright red car
to the other's funeral,
or what think is the other's funeral.

76078342R00031